MW00365491

POEMS, RHYMES & REAL

HEARTFELT STUFF II

George Tedesco

authorHOUSE®

AuthorHouse™
1663 Liberty Drive
Bloomington, IN 47403
www.authorhouse.com
Phone: 1 (800) 839-8640

Published by AuthorHouse 06/22/2020

ISBN: 978-1-7283-6547-3 (sc)
ISBN: 978-1-7283-6548-0 (e)

Print information available on the last page.

This book is printed on acid-free paper.

Because of the dynamic nature of the Internet, any web
addresses or links contained in this book may have changed
since publication and may no longer be valid. The views
expressed in this work are solely those of the author and do
not necessarily reflect the views of the publisher, and the
publisher hereby disclaims any responsibility for them.

Contents

Introduction

Well it looks like you're back for more fun, light poetry and that's fantastic. This is the fifth publication of the *"Poems, Rhymes & Real..."* book series and I couldn't be happier.

I was sitting in the kitchen listening to Silver Chair's "Tomorrow", such a great song, drinking a cup of coffee, thinking whether or not I should write a fifth 'poem' book. A lot goes into it, more than most would think. That small poem that appeared so simple in design, had 45 other versions that were thrown away. Besides trying to keep your topics, ideas and words light and fresh, non-offensive and not too controversial, (cuz who needs those problems... not this guy) it's a constant scrutiny and dissection from yourself, not to mention the never ending couch critics online.

Any writer will tell you, writing can be therapeutic, even cathartic. Your work becomes a diary of thoughts and beliefs, inspirations and dreams and deep emotions. Including heavy personal losses and to bring up those losses and other painful memories, can be emotionally exhausting to revisit. I've found myself in tears more than a few times; specifically missing my daughter, my brother, my father, sorting through mistakes I've made, along with events others have brought on that are completely out of my control. Don't get me wrong, I've had a lot of good things happen to me, but I've also had my fair share of deep soul scarring sadness, tragedy and bullshit. So again, I asked myself, do you want to go through all that again? And the answer hit me on the last sip of my vanilla creamer infused, freshly ground brew...

No.

I then walked upstairs to my laptop and told myself "I'm just opening it up. Don't worry, I'm not going to get lost in writing. I'm not doing it."

And yet here we are. Honestly, I love all my books dearly and I'm very proud of them for many reasons. Since I started this endeavor, I've learned there are many different types of poetry. First and foremost, it's how the writer sees expression. That being said, my hope is that you simply enjoy what I've written as much as I do. This looks to be my last book of this series, so I'm excited to leave you with this fifth and final compilation. Thank you from the bottom of my heart for reading. Take care of your family, be safe, be good to each other and love poetry! I'm George and these are my poems.

*Poems, Rhymes & Real Heartfelt Sh*t

**Poems, Passages & Real Heartfelt Sh*t

***Poems, Rhymes & Real Foul Mouthed Sh*t

****Poems, Rhymes & Real Heartfelt Stuff

*****Poems, Rhymes & Real Heartfelt Stuff II

Facade

Hiding behind protective facades,
we mask the depths of where pain lingers.
Eyes stand guard, stabbing forward,
keep the crowd moving and repelling visitors.
But the soul peeks through its gated view,
screaming to be free and recognized.
The reflection never lies
as the heart streams live.
I wonder if anyone else
can see me inside.

Poisonous Roots

Trees wonderfully exceed their reach,
expanding their dreams,
seeking warmth from the sun,
existing just to give all life oxygen.
They produce fruit and seed that fill the need
and feed the beings that survive off it's nourishment,
but upon closer dissection,
infection and diseased leaves all around
plague the entities existence,
animals tear away at it's core without resistance,
draining it's life and spilling its blood,
rotting the roots where it grew
so heartily from mud.

The forest is in devastation.
Suffering spreads through all creation.

I Believe

I believe,
not by force or by screaming, just thinking within
reason, that every breathing being, whether creature
that crawls, walks or talks, has the right to be free
and find out how high it can fly before it dies.
We should be nestling in dreams, knee deep in
streams, soaring through clouds, not wondering if
we're allowed, but admiring, creating, giving all we
can to succeed in what we individually believe.
But there's a catch;
We work as a team.
I mean, that's why we're here. That's what we fear, to
be alone before we're covered in stone, thrown into the
ocean, back to the unknown as sinking ash and bone.
With the same destination, it shouldn't be so hard
to have consideration and come together as one,
to help one another under one sun.

Maybe it's just me, but that's what I believe.

Last Request

She asked me,
"Daddy, if you had one wish, what would it
be?"I thought carefully about the words that
have always been golden to her ears.
"To always be with you my love.
To watch you grow up free of pain, see your wings
unfold and become the beauty that was your mother.
To watch you try. Fail or succeed it doesn't matter to
me, because you'd always have me to lift you up and
brush off your knee and give you the advice you need
to help you understand, you only get one life to be all
you can be, so reach for the stars, but be happy."
She looked at me with sad eyes and
knew that could never be.
**These were my last words to her as
my final minutes are upon me.
Dear God, please watch over my daughter for m**

Inherited

Is there purpose to plan or
just madness without mend?
And what of the children?
Do we tell them we failed?
We've done little to change the world around them.
In fact, disaster sits in waiting,
with precious time fading.
We've left nothing to inherit but a lifetime stained
in mistakes, deeply engraved in pain.
Forsaken landscapes drained of their intended destiny.
Lists of dreams and promises lie stacked
in the debris of arrogance and stupidity,
missed chances and lack of humility.

We've let ourselves and our world become
broken and shattered.
But does any of that even matter?
At this rate, time itself will be the judge and will
overcome it all sooner than later, washing us away,
and in our decay, one question will remain,

What have we done with all of our days?

Anchors

Anchors drown.
It's their purpose to hold you down.
If...
within breathing your thoughts suffocate,
within sleeping, your dreams become tainted
and overtake your most peaceful state,
it may be time to free your sails of the line
that's dragging you under,
and cut the dead weight.

Still

The year has changed,
but my feelings haven't.
I still love the same things I did as a young boy
and I'm still just as passionate.
Cookies and milk, an adventure in a good book,
I still cherish those miniature moments most overlook.

I still hold the dream that you can be what you want,
eat what you love, play long into the night, shake
hands without regret, have a family for life,
do what is right without fear of what might...
and I still believe you can fall in love
if you wholeheartedly try.

Resurrection

An unfathomable pain
takes the place of anything sane.
Even breathing has to be relearned again.
So you've lost your way, become a ghost and a slave.
Now who's to blame if you don't get up and change?
Anymore time and love lost is dictated through
how swiftly you regain and restore.
Resurrect your inner self and be the
strength you once were and more.

Selfish Seamstress

Slowly dismantled, layer by layer.
Calculatingly handled, cut by cut.
Your grand design, to her entrusted,
carefully, she weaves her puppet.
Taken apart piece by piece,
stitched seams are now gashed open.
Threads that once held you together
were systematically cut to her fashion,
perfectly spilling out your dreams,
losing everything that meant anything
by what feels like the world's most selfish being.

Rock Solid

Rock solid I am to be,
for I have children in my life that need me.
I met a beautiful woman that loves me.
You don't have to tell me I'm lucky.
So I have no time for pain and worry,
nevertheless...
I'll work til my last bone cracks.
Hug them all til the world stops spinning.
Care for them like a man obsessed.
This is what my father defined as "Winning."

"Fight for them, cry for them,
even die for them if you have to.
Blood or not, they are your family.
This is how it's supposed to be.
You're a man.
Be one for all to envy."

Brightside of Dark II

I'm aggravated, I'm bored, I'm broke and I'm tired.
I'm sick, got the virus, I'm fed up and yeah, I even got fired.
I've been stepped on, used, backstabbed and
betrayed. Let's not forget, let go, cheated
on, ignored and eternally frustrated.

But...
I'm sober. I'm clean.
Alive to see my children dream.
I made it this far and I haven't run out of steam.
I have five great kids in my life and there's
always room in my heart for more.
I've had riches and cars and laughed
til I fell on the floor.
I'm loved by friends and family and I have their respect
I'm told. My word is gold.
I'm proud that I've spent a lifetime putting others first.
Times can definitely be a little tough.
Sounds like life on planet Earth.

U.S. Brother

Barely a man, back from his tour
lost in the torment of his world,
scared and alone, scarred to the bone
still figuring out the meaning of life.
Just scraping by,
choking on bills of every kind,
had children he wasn't ready for,
overwhelmed and war-torn,
he carried burdens so big it could
throw any man off his stride.
Looking to dull the pain with the meds they
gave him, he ran to the shadows to hide.
He accidentally took too much
and of course they betrayed and took his life.

As I stood over his grave, the world never felt colder.
I often think how much I miss him;
my brother, the father, the uncle, the soldier.

(Dedicated to Marc Tedesco)

Sweet Embrace

Cheerfully inviting,
simply enticing,
thoughtfully caring in so many ways.
The curves of her smile melt me,
comfortably telling me,
forget what you've gone through
and come breathe again.
Her eyes whisper,
"I'm all yours, love me, as I do you."
Perfect, in every aspect,
putting others before herself,
she's fought off the forces that crept
while building a future on promises kept.
It's the things she says when she holds my face,
It's the way she pulls me close by my waist.
Her soothing kiss intoxicates, electrifying the chase.
But most of all,
it's how she saved my soul,
from misery's dark cold,
with her warm, sweet embrace.

Moments

It is said that our existence is but a moment in time,
and smaller moments are the canvases of our lives,
that we should paint our crazy dreams and
magnificent scenes into them with every stroke
we have before those moments pass us by.

Like blue skies that arrive and inspire
or that random campfire with friends new and old,
play whenever you get that chance
with all your heart and soul.
Before the sun sets on your day,
before you're face up in a grave,
cherish, rejoice and savor the memories made.
For it was in those moments that your life took place.

Now or Never

I tell myself to never surrender.
Remind myself to get it together
Don't fall to the negativity of the era.
Never give up on things you'll regret in the mirror.
And remember,
we all have to keep our heads above water.
Too much at stake to just sit in a corner
wasting our lives, sidelined by comments so
quick to fly from mouths that no doubt,
have no idea what their talking about.
Unfortunately, on wings of misfortune we must ride,
accidentally or gallantly, willingly or reluctantly
it's your call how you embrace this endeavor,
but either way, it's now or never.

Death's Revenge

With heavy sword drawn,
I kicked open the thick wooden door of the musky tavern.
Rushing to fill my nostrils were
the smells of stale ale, pipe ash and sour men.
My hands gripped tighter as I sharpened my focus.
Drinking and stacking coins was their version of business.
Few gazed at my scowl. Some stared at my steel.
They all knew by the look of vengeance in my eyes,
why I was there, would soon be revealed.

The macabre scene was still fresh in vision.
Her bloody position, his home torn to pieces. All he had
worked for was taken, his wife raped and beaten. Her last
breath in whisper spoke of the vicious attack that took her.
Their life long plans and all of their
dreams now lost, and gone forever.
"I could kill every last one of you
and the world would be that much brighter.
You're no different than the animals that crawl,
or the spawn of Hell's fire.
Remember these words. Someone will pay,
for all they've taken from me today."
"Claudia?"
A voice shockingly mumbled from the corner
"YES! MY CLAUDIA!"
SAY HER NAME. NOW KNOW MINE.
To you, I am Death. Fear me when you sleep,
and again when you wake. I will hunt you down and
avenge her death til my bones and sword doth break.
For if you see me, it'll be too late. You'll already be
dead, walking through the gates of Hell, looking at
me through the eyes of your greedy severed head."

(to be continued)

H.B.I.C

(Head Bullshitter in Charge)

Word twister, time waster, sin spitter, two-
sided shape shifting bullshitter.
Oh how you play games with our lives, hitting
us where it hurts, playing on our emotions
like an evil twin sister, a fantastic grifter.
Tricking our minds, weaving webs of lies for the blind,
designed to lure us into bed, poisoning our heads
with deceptive tactics, psycho babble antics, painting
a planned canvas, like we're from damn Kansas.
Speaking as though we can't see right through you
and your thin veil of well-worded voodoo.
You double talk and backtrack, set us up for
the backstab, all the while with a smile
where you don't even seem half bad,
but who knows?
It's like a grab bag.

You sit in your high chair as if we're unaware
of the monetary share you get from caressing
our wants of the fair share we're entitled to.
Shame on you and your fictitious missions,
because you have no plan to put us in a
position where we can make decisions.
You rather keep us locked in this prison.

Deepest Regret

Worn out paths, bring back the past.
Memories made, unknowingly lasted.
Standing on old grounds, hearing old sounds,
remembering old friends, deeply missed,
a painfully, sad, reminisce.
I can't remember exactly when I lost touch.
I've forgotten so many and so much,
everything inspiring,
everything that made my being lively.
Why did I quit being happy?
The hell's wrong with me.

Fuel

With every second passing
time advances,
costing me precious moments and priceless chances,
amassing my debt of heavy regret.
Goals to which I aspire but never reach,
leave receipts of empty dreams, piling higher
along the streets of my desire.

Time waits for no man, for no plan.
Some say,
"The skies not the limit, it's just a view."
Reach for the dreams that keep you awake at night.
Reach for the stars that align and define your life.

Don't let your time expire with goals unadmired
to become the fuel for your own funeral pyre.

The Woods of Agor

Cast out, shackled and banished,
sent off to die in the woods of Agor.
Many nights with hands locked in heavy bondage,
the accused suffered for what he stood for.
He was warned not to speak his mind so freely, don't
speak of the oppressed, the wicked or the tyranny.
Stick to picking your crops, do as you're
commanded, ignore the conspiracy.
Be grateful you're handed the life you live, the little
things they let you have, for you are nothing without
wealth and power. Kneel. Be silent and cower.

Tarin believed there was more. He was more than happy
to be banished to Agor. With his heart leading the way
through storms and frigid nights, starvation and fights,
he finally came to a village with wonderful sounds and
lights. They unbound his hands and restored his rights.
"Welcome to Agor. You are no longer under rule.
You're free to speak your ideas and more.
Your life is a gift, be happy you were born.
No creature or man should suffer,
No one is born better. Talents are to be discovered.
Hatred is to be surrendered. Now go mingle with
the others, there are many who believe in love
and will support your happiness my brother.
For Agor stands for
the **A**ge where man **G**ave all life a chance
Over the idea of **R**uling.
Here, we lead with fresh ideas and the freedom to
speak. There's no jealousy, hatred, or greed.

We work together as a team to feed, care
and be free to chase our dreams, preventing
stagnant thinking and eternal suffering.

There Tarin lived happily til he passed in his sleep
at the age of 83.

Right Side Up

My life is not where I belong.
My love is always thrown around.
My world is never what I thought,
it's always upside down.

What if my life is exactly where the
good lord wanted it to be?
What if I'm exactly where I belong, to
inspire the ones around me.
What if my love is thrown around because
so many need what I can give.
Maybe I should stop thinking what my life *should* be...
and realize it's right side up, purposely.

Wings

Designed to fly or so I thought.
They're still there, just not showing signs of life.
I've waited a long time for them to take me where I want.
It's possible I've misjudged my reach
and the heights that I could achieve.
It's possible my wings weren't meant for flight,
that they're meant to fan out the fires
I leave behind.

Too Much

Misunderstand me, be upset with me,
but it's all spilt milk, unintentionally.
Gradually, like rising seas
patience will lead us to a warmer place.
Maybe we just need a moment, a phrase,
a sentimental gaze,
perhaps I could clean up this place,
kiss that face, set up our favorite game,
or make a few bad jokes at my own expense.
Anything to get you to smile and believe,
I'm sorry.
Sometimes I can be too much, even for me.

Transport II

Crystal streams speak to the morning breeze.
Orange and green tree tops sway high above
their fallen leaves.
I stoke the crackling wood fire by the lake's edge.
The smell of smoke and food rise
higher, waking up the kids.

I see this in my dreams.
A beautiful scenery possibly camping with a family.
Personally, I'm tired of being alone. Tired of not
having a home, tired of the lies constantly told.
Tired of being used, being cold and getting old.

I know this isn't the life god wanted for me.
So sick of looking at streets that don't want me.
Everyone has left me.
My biggest fear is dying without making
something of myself, finding a place to call
home and going to sleep without a family.

<u>Fears</u>

"I remember the good ole days when my biggest
fears were the dark and monsters under my bed."

I replied to my friend and said,

"Try being close to 50, losing your job and
the place to permanently lay your head.
Try having children with women who take them so
far away, you'll never get to tuck them into bed.
Try slaving away for decades and a day,
but your bank account seems permanently
stuck at zero.

Then forever watch your phone, hoping your daughter
will call like she did when she was small,
when she called you her hero.

I still have fears to blame,
it's just now the monsters have changed."

Deaf, Dumb & Blind

Cliche cries stain the night.
Masses march on with fire and fight.
Chanting their demands, assuming rights, naivety
commands while poisonous fingers blame and point.

Blind is the man who finds fault in
everyone else but himself.
Deaf is the man who only hears his own words
in depth.
&
Ignorance of the pain you cause doesn't make you exempt.

Our Song

Open your heart, open your mind,
open your hands to me.
Open your world, come on inside, you'll find me here.
Give me everything you are and I'll give you all of me.

Unconditionally.

Do you remember when we first kissed,
next to the evergreens.
You laughed and held onto me
like you knew you'd love me.

For eternity.

You're all I've ever wanted. All I've ever asked for.
You're that. . . and so much more.

A Guiding Light

Through cloudy skies, restless nights
and twisted vines that climb past patience,
draining resistance, pushing limits,
and testing heights of stations
inside heart and mind, she finds, illuminates
and decorates with magnificent design.
Carefully filling crevices where darkness resides
as the guiding light
of my life.

Soul Drain

I have let the cold creep in.
I have let the gloom seep in.
I have been the victim of succumbing to the black.
Waiting for the clock, fearing the dark,
giving into madness,
sleeping with enemies of the heart.

I fell to jealousy, chaos and rage within,
I let mechanical termites dig way in.
I became enslaved by the game handcrafted to make me
think I was insane and needed to give more than they.

All I can do now is pray.

Maybe I should've done more of that along the way,
instead of wasting precious time,
catering to everyone and everything that takes.

Traction

Walking through miles of twisted,
cursed desert earth.
I'm outta breath and still fighting off death.
There's no shelter from the antithesis of adventure,
just immeasurable lecture from the burning,
truth-telling, reality of gravity and ground
that points out how
I chose the wrong path to go down.
The road is trampled, but not paved.
The way is complimented with ornaments of pain,
complicating the maps I've made.
I'm hyperventilating without change.
I'm praying for rain.
Maybe a new day will give me a clean slate
to draw up the plans that'll help me erase the footsteps
I've laid in the sands where no traction can be made.

Spit and Filth

Hate
betrays the gates of life eternal,
twisting the way we grow, hunching us over.
Greedily feeding on the emotional breakdown
of another. Tempering demonic viciousness
and it's piss into humanity's bloodline for the
vengeful destruction of our own kind.
A cruel and deadly concoction carried out
with gloating satisfaction,
painfully corrupting truth and love with
disruption, misdirection and menacing action.
Seething anger blooms, tears ignored.
Hysteria cannot erect it's towers of chaos without a
power-trip of conflict and unnecessary discord.

The words you spit and the filth you give
dig the hellish pit where you deserve to live.

Say Something Cool

Temp me, lure me, pull me in deep.
Envelop me with those words I wanna hear.
Tickle my passion with affection.
Wake me up from this long winters sleep.
I admire your eyes and the cute way you sit by my side,
I'm willing to go that extra mile, anytime, day or night,
but,
Entice me, bite me, electrify me with your lightning.
We only live once they say.
Well I've lived a thousand boring lifetimes filled
with lies and dead tales of why, with people that just
aren't grateful for my time. Promises that were the
fumes or mere settling dust from misplaced lust.
So speak to me. Dig deep with dreams, or
even tenderly, but don't just sit there.
Hell, give it to me.
I'm a man who loves all of you.
That's why I call for you.
Wasting our time, only makes you the fool.
Say something cool.

Praying for Rain

There once was a saying;

*"When it drizzles, it's a sign that God is crying.
When there's thunder, it's another, where he's angry."*

But the saying doesn't mention the next part;

"When it pours."

For when it pours, God is doing all he can to cleanse and
wash away the madness that festers, the sickness that
lingers, and the never ending sadness that has fallen
on mankind's existence because of his ignorance.

Then comes a new day, where the sun rises brightly,
shining intently, warming hearts ever so gently,
removing the weight of doubt and filling them with
hope and the strength to lift the spirit back up,
casting out darkness, replacing it with guidance.

A cloudy day is a sign of forgiveness
and a way to put the past behind us.
I *pray* for the rains to find us.

Simple Moments

Simple moments turn into magical memories
As our lives affectionately intertwine.

We grasp desperately to find another of our kind
while avoiding the brutal mistakes that can be
so easily made by a worn-out soul inside.

There are moments when the world quiets down
And the ride seems less frightening, even calming, in
fact, slightly exciting even though we're not moving,
It's in those simple moments when it all becomes clear,
where I'm not crippled with hopelessness and fear.

It's our embrace that softens the blow from the
fights we've fought on our individual roads.

It's in the seconds we take to stare into each
other's soul that heal the wounds and stole what
was left of our hearts as we stood alone.
It's in your voice that i have found the answers I've
needed, the deeper meaning, to the journey
I've made so far.

Thank You

I've spent years running away from you.
I know that sounds odd, but it's true.
Pathetic? Possibly.
Maybe even wrong of me to do.
You introduced me to falling in love
and so many other incredible things that would
burrow deep into my heart and shake my soul,
woke my whole being, even showed me I had feelings.

And then, just like that, you left me.
I had never felt more alone.
Hurt, betrayed, lost my purpose and was
truly brokenhearted to the bone.
The world kept on spinning and left me behind.
I was so hurt, I buried everything about you
I could find,
banishing you deep into the corners of my mind.

Years later,
I was once again, standing in that same dark
familiar territory, and you somehow came back to me.
And then I saw with my own eyes
how you took care of me.
Seems like you never forgot me.

I'm not even sure you ever left me.

Thank you for blessing me.

Death's Revenge
part II

Having nowhere else to go,
I returned to my house up the road.
Upon entering my home, I noticed
darkness and gloom had taken over the once
warm and lively, sweetly scented room.
No more daffodils floating in watery vases or
warm pumpkin pies fresh out the oven.
The light of this house had gone out when the
love of my life was sent back to heaven.
I was alone with my thoughts.
Do I challenge life again or disappear far, of course
after I hunt down the demon who took Claudia's life.
My love. My soulmate. My wife.
My chair had never felt so uncomfortable.
For why should it be?
How could I ever rest or relax after
what was done to my Claudia?
I picked up my bag for travel and for
the last time I looked around.
That's when I knew it all had to be burned down,
all the way to the ground.
And that's when I saw the medallion.
It was under the table next to some broken ornaments.
To my shock and horror it was a medallion
of the armed regiments!
Soldiers we trusted! They are supposed to be the
protectors of the lands, not murderous thieves
who prey on the weak and do as they please!

With no apologies,
my existence was shattered.
No one can bring back or change what was lost.
They took a life as if it didn't matter.
And for that, there must be a cost.

Daddy Issue

Strong as I may seem,
doesn't mean,
I don't have weaknesses that cripple.
Even in dream,
I face demons in battle.
Everyday I struggle
to be more than I was yesterday,
to succeed past dreams and make it further
than my father.
Personally, I'm afraid to get older
without inspiring my son's and daughters.
Unsuccessful attempts and failure
to reach the next step
don't make me as bad as my father was. . .
lack of trying over and over does.

Devastated

A vile display with aggravating decay,
buckle and betray an already wounded nation.
Years in the making, a massive undertaking,
brought down in minutes from
a snake infestation with poisonous resolution,
filling the cracks of great halls, weakening walls
with slithering coil strikes and greedy solutions.
Innocent lives lost, a perpetual blood loss.
Victims cry out in mass desperation.
A grand scale of separation.
Fingers point in every direction.
United we stand in devastation.

Super Fly

She's
selflessly romantic and thoughtfully warm,
accidentally seductive and playfully coy.
She's enchanting to say the least.
classically funny with an innocent twist;
honest and pure, with a knock-out kiss.
Her eyes tell a story you wanna be in,
leaving depths to explore,
sharing everything.
She is all anyone could ever ask for.
She sings like an angel and dances like the devil,
loves hard, letting nothing bother her.
She's beyond beautiful, inside and out.
Even her laugh,
is just sexy as hell.
and yes. . . I could be,
most definitely, under her spell.

She's the complete definition of woman,
in my eyes.
She's just so cool. So Super Fly.

Shameless

This is what we made.
A span between healing and grief is
where we seem to stay.
Apparently, it's our belief to perpetuate the feeling,
desecrate our being, and capitalize on
lying, stealing and cheating.
We brutalize, disguising our own breath,
setting fire to our own mess, even if it brings death
to the doorstep of innocence.
We live a selfish, remorseless existence.
Instead of picking up the pieces of what's left
and be responsible for our own mistakes,
we rather point and blame.
We rather spread more pain.
We haven't a single ounce of shame.
Just as long as there's monetary gain.

The Abyss

Into the abyss I sink.
My heart pounds like never before.
My body aches, the deeper I go.
I know I'll survive, but doubt weighs heavily
on my mind,
especially with the unforeseeable.
Why am I still holding on, even tethered
to this sinking ship that's unretrievable.
She's gone. Let her go. Move on.
Let yourself float back up to the top.
Take in some fresh air and breathe again.
They'll be other ships to set sail in.

My Daughters

Not a day goes by
without a thought why;
why I've given all I have inside.

Not a minute has passed where
new heights haven't been climbed.
I've reached for the stars at night, just so they'd
have a shining light to guide their way,
so they'd know
what it was like to have a fathers love
follow them everyday.
My only regret
is that I'll die before I can defend their last day.
So I've hand crafted shadows to walk beside them
and watch their back, even on sunny days.

Pointless Obsession

Motionless gestures. Empty promises.
Careening beliefs over instant pleasures.
Selfishness at peak levels.
Disregard for needs that feed
emotional streams, cutting off dreams.
Visibly attacking us where we bleed,
but inside we scream to be free.
We need to be free.
We're drowning in oceans of pain,
catastrophically dying in vein.
Why do we feel the need to sacrifice our entire existence
for a moment of attention, or a collection of
worthless possessions that'll only bury
all of our good intentions.
We're so much better
than this obsession.

The Last Epiphany of Man

We have the potential. We all are essential,
and with solidarity we've proven we're unstoppable.
We dream deeper, fly farther, aspire to climb higher,
even put our lives in danger to reach for the victories
that'll reshape and design our lives for the better.
Not just for our own good,
but for others to see we'll fight for their endeavors,
now and forever.
Let's save each other.
No more buckling under pressure.
No more crying alone in a corner.
We already work harder, now it's time to think smarter.
Our generation can be the epiphany of man
as we make this last stand to reverse the
polarity of outrage and abnormality.
Outlaw the catalyst of sorrow, rewrite and prevent
these atrocities and horrors.
Weed out all the snakes in the garden
and let's stand together
to rebuild our children a new tomorrow.
God Bless

CPSIA information can be obtained
at www.ICGtesting.com
Printed in the USA
BVHW040740160720
583853BV00010B/135